Nuno Almeida
Mário Teixeira
João Pereira

DIRECTION AND MANAGEMENT OF HEALTH & FITNESS CLUBS

Nuno Almeida
Mário Teixeira
João Pereira

DIRECTION AND MANAGEMENT OF HEALTH & FITNESS CLUBS

Analysis of business management strategies and services of fitness clubs

ScienciaScripts

Imprint

Any brand names and product names mentioned in this book are subject to trademark, brand or patent protection and are trademarks or registered trademarks of their respective holders. The use of brand names, product names, common names, trade names, product descriptions etc. even without a particular marking in this work is in no way to be construed to mean that such names may be regarded as unrestricted in respect of trademark and brand protection legislation and could thus be used by anyone.

Cover image: www.ingimage.com

This book is a translation from the original published under ISBN 978-620-2-80805-7.

Publisher:
Sciencia Scripts
is a trademark of
International Book Market Service Ltd., member of OmniScriptum Publishing Group
17 Meldrum Street, Beau Bassin 71504, Mauritius
Printed at: see last page
ISBN: 978-620-3-39795-6

Copyright © Nuno Almeida, Mário Teixeira, João Pereira
Copyright © 2021 International Book Market Service Ltd., member of OmniScriptum Publishing Group

THANKS

The realization of this dissertation relied on several supports, without which its realization would have been possible.

First of all, I want to thank my supervisors, Prof. Mário Teixeira and Prof. Nuno Almeida for all their support, example, and professionalism.

I would also like to thank my parents, Maria Valente, my brother, and Mafalda Sousa for all the support throughout this dissertation, for all the encouragement, encouragement, patience, understanding, affection, encouragement, and advice.

Finally, I would like to thank everyone who participated in filling out the questionnaires and thus made this study possible.

To all, my enormous thanks.

DIRECTION AND MANAGEMENT OF HEALTH & FITNESS CLUBS

Analysis of fitness clubs' business and service management strategies

SUMMARY

With the increase in social awareness of the benefits of physical activity, gyms have begun to invest in new techniques to increase the number of people interested in their services.

The purpose of this study is to gather information in order to understand (1) the attributes provided by the gym; (2) the environment and competence of the employees; (3) other ancillary attributes designed to please the customer.

The information was collected through surveys of the managing bodies and users of health clubs in Portugal.

It was concluded that customers give preference to the cleanliness conditions, the friendliness and competence of the staff, the opening hours and the environment in the gym. Managers need to improve these conditions for their customers so that they will frequent the health club more often and thus remain loyal for more years at their gym. It was found that preferences and degrees of satisfaction can change according to the seniority of the customer in the health club.

Keywords: sports management; sports marketing; strategy; health clubs.

GENERAL INDEX

TABLE OF CONTENTS

TABLE OF FIGURES

LIST OF ABBREVIATIONS

PTs - Personal trainers

Etc - Etcétera

CHAPTER I - INTRODUCTION

1.1 Framework of the theme

Due to the increased social awareness of the benefits of physical activity, which plays an extremely relevant role in the promotion of a healthy lifestyle (Fernandes & Pereira, 2006), there has been an increase in the number of people interested in attending sports venues. According to the Fitness Barometer in Portugal 2018, there was a 23% increase in the number of registrants in 2016 and in 2018 it increased by 17% (Pedragosa & Cardadeiro, 2018). In parallel, this has led to an increase in the number of gyms available, as, according to the 2016 Fitness Barometer in Portugal research team, the number of gym openings increased by 14% in 2016 (Moreira, Cardadeiro, & Pedragosa, 2016)increasing competitiveness in the sector and leading existing gyms to invest in new techniques to increase the number of people interested in their gym. This factor forces the managing entities to a more precise and careful administration. Therefore, it is important to know and study which factors, strategies and characteristics of gyms work best in order to enhance new spaces and for a better management and profitability of existing gyms.

There is a set of specific characteristics for the sport that force managers to adapt and consider new management practices under penalty of them not having good results (Sá & Sá, 2009). For a good management of a gym it is also necessary to know the characteristics of consumers and what they are looking for, because the sports consumer also awakens some particularities that must be taken into account.

This study aims to obtain information about the Health Club, its customers and their priorities as consumers in a space for the practice of sport and physical activity. Thus, there will be a study of sports marketing which is currently an important management tool in any sports organization, because it contains a set of techniques, from market research to advertising and public relations, based on a management that is based on the group of sports customers interested in the company's services (Valinhas, 2010).

1.2 Aims

The purpose of this study is to understand the main reasons why people prefer a certain gym. After understanding and analyzing these reasons related to customer satisfaction, managers can adopt favorable strategies for their gym.

The purpose of this study is then to obtain relevant information through surveys of users and managers of gyms and/or other spaces intended exclusively for sports practice, so as to be able to understand which strategies increase customer retention and satisfaction, as well as greater profitability of the space. This objective is therefore to analyze (1) the marketing and profitability strategies of the gyms; (2) the training methodologies put into practice; (3) other accessory attributes aimed at pleasing the customer.

1.3 Motivations and relevance of the study

In the scope of the master's degree course in sports management and direction, this dissertation focuses on analyzing the management strategies of health clubs in Portugal, specifically in the north of Continental Portugal.

The current relevance and increasing interest of the population in health clubs generated motivation to move forward with this master's project.

1.4 Structure and organization of the research

This dissertation is structured in eight chapters.

The first chapter houses the framework of the topic, the objectives of the study, the motivations and relevance of the study, and the research structure and organization.

Chapter II contains the literature review. This chapter serves to contextualize the importance of marketing in this study. Focusing on sports marketing, relational marketing and services in the fitness industry. Management strategies in health clubs are also discussed.

Reading the third chapter explains the methodology used in this research, where the methods of data collection and analysis are mentioned.

In chapter IV comes the formulation of hypotheses, which are framed bibliographically according to the issues analyzed.

The presentation of results appears in chapter V, and here the most pertinent results are analyzed. In chapter VI, with the help of the information analyzed in the previous chapter, the hypotheses are analyzed and validated.

Chapter VII describes the main conclusions concerning this study, the limitations of this study, and suggestions for future research.

Finally, chapter VIII will show the bibliographical references that were used in this dissertation.

CHAPTER II - LITERATURE REVIEW

2.1 Marketing

Until the late 20th century, sales activities were seen as secondary to production. The content of marketing was limited to sales, physical distribution, and advertising. But thanks to the emergence of mass production marketing became more prominent, making its content broader, from conception to sale, extending its field of application to industrial goods, banks, churches, newspapers, political parties, among others (Valinhas, 2010).

The concept of marketing has been evolving due to increased competition (Marinho, 2011) and also due to the technological and digital revolutions that have taken place in recent decades. These changes have completely transformed marketing practice, consumer behavior, and competitive dynamics (Moorman, Heerde, Moreau, & Palmatier, 2019). Marketing aims to promote, through various methods, behaviors that assist the achievement of an organization's objectives (Londrevie, Dionísio, Denis, & Rodrigues, 1996).

For Kotler (2000), marketing is a social and managerial process where people get what they want through the development and exchange of products and services. That is, it is the development of exchanges in which companies and customers engage voluntarily in transactions that benefit both (Churchill Jr & Peter, 2017). Hence it is said that marketing is an exchange relationship, because it only exists when a company has something to offer the market (Ferreira, Marques, Caetano, Rasquilha, & Rodrigues, 2015). To make successful exchanges, marketers analyze what each party expects from the transaction (Kotler, 2000). Two parties are involved in an exchange when they are negotiating, that is, when they are trying to find mutually acceptable terms, and after these are found, the transaction takes place (Kotler, 2000).

Marketing, according to the American Marketing Association (2017), is "*the activity, set of institutions, and processes to create, communicate, deliver, and exchange offerings that have value to consumers, customers, partners, and society at large.* " These definitions show the breadth of the concept. In other words, the focus of marketing is not only selling products to customers, it is also generating value, studying the market, understanding and building customer loyalty, and increasing the company's image, thus becoming stronger in the market.

Regardless of all existing definitions of marketing, there is always a common point: the behavior towards the market and the activities designed to reach the customer. These activities are, for example, market research, adaptation of products and/or services to the customer, pricing and promotion of the product and/or service (Ferreira, Marques, Caetano, Rasquilha, & Rodrigues, 2015).

Market research is the identification, collection and analysis of information in a systematic way with the objective of improving decisions regarding problem identification and solution (Zamberlan, 2008).

The adjustment of the product and/or service is very important because this adjustment is part of the strategic planning that should direct the company to a good level of quality. To improve the product and/or service it is necessary, first, to identify the customers, their needs and desires (Cardoso, 1995). A product is something that can satisfy a need or a desire and it will be successful in the market if it delivers value and satisfaction to the customer (Kotler, 2000).

The sales price of a product consists of calculating the costs plus the contribution margin (Sepp, Manfroi, Theisen, Diel, & Diel, 2015). The contribution margin is the difference between the sales price and the variable cost (Dias, 1992), that is, it is what is left for the organization to pay fixed expenses and generate profit. (Junior, Bruni, Paixão, & Filho, 2009). The ideal price is considered to be the one that, by covering the costs of production and sales of the product, and also containing the expected profit percentage, allows the company to maintain a competitive position in the market. The setting of sales prices of products and/or services affects the company daily, regardless of its size, its products or its economic sector, because it influences the production chain (Sepp, Manfroi, Theisen, Diel, & Diel, 2015). Besides that, the manager must also analyze the internal factors and the behavior of the market where it is inserted (Lopes, Matos, & Moraes, 1999).

Promotion exists when the company communicates and advertises its products and/or services to customers. Promotion also exists when the organization promotes the company as a whole (Pelsmacker, Geuens, & Bergh, 2010). The tools that can be used in promotion are, for example: advertising, direct marketing communications, sales, public relations, personal selling and sponsorships (Rowley, 1998).

Advertising is one of the oldest, most visible and most important tools of marketing as it is crucial to inform and persuade customers and potential customers (Pelsmacker, Geuens, & Bergh, 2010). This tool is a paid way of promoting an idea, goods or services, carried out by the company, which is aided by the use of mass communication media such as television, radio or newspapers. (Pelsmacker, Geuens, & Bergh, 2010).

Direct marketing communications is a marketing tool where the goal is to reach customers and potential customers in a personal and direct way. Flyers, telemarketing actions, e-mails, among others are ways to use this marketing tool (Pelsmacker, Geuens, & Bergh, 2010).

Sales are campaigns that stimulate sales to convince customers that they need the product. During sales periods salesmen focus on achieving short-term results for their companies (Weitz & Bradford, 1999). These campaigns can be, for example: price reductions, coupons, or free samples. (Pelsmacker, Geuens, & Bergh, 2010).

Public relations involves a variety of programs that are designed to promote a company's image and products (Kotler, 2000). In addition public relations also helps to identify, establish and maintain mutually beneficial relationships between a company and the various publics on which its success or failure depends (Kitchen & Moss, 1995).

Personal selling is a way to present and demonstrate the product and/or service orally to potential customers (Pelsmacker, Geuens, & Bergh, 2010).

Sponsorship exists when the sponsor provides funds, goods, services or *know-how*. The sponsored company will thus obtain a reinforcement of its brand, and in this way will strengthen its market position (Pelsmacker, Geuens, & Bergh, 2010).

2.1.1 Sports Marketing

Marketing is currently part of the sports lexicon, however, twenty years ago, in Portugal, it was an unknown theme for most sports agents. The whole development of sport was centered on the support of the State, which was in charge of promoting it to the population. Only relatively recently has marketing reached the world of sport (Paulico, 2008).

In the last half of the twentieth century, reality was strongly modified since sport has achieved great popularity and relevance, both in as much as the practice is concerned and in as much as the follow up of events of sporting nature by the public is concerned. Thus, it is normal to classify sport as a business due to the economic, financial and social impact of the sporting phenomenon (Paulico, 2008).

Sports marketing has as its main goal to satisfy the needs and expectations of a consumer related to sports. This concept can be divided into two sectors, i.e. there is the marketing of sports products and services, which relate to the customer. And the marketing that uses the sport to promote their products and / or services, and may or may not have a connection with the sport (Afif, 2000).

Sports marketing is in practice when a sports product and/or service that is needed or desired by clients is identified, planned, programmed and developed. These, which by becoming more demanding and more complex, have led to the need for companies operating in the sports market to adopt an attitude aimed at satisfying their needs. Another important feature is the fact that consumers in this market are very sensitive to emotional factors and their relationship with sport, for example through their favorite athlete or team. (Paulico, 2008). The disclosure, promotion and sale of this sports product and/or service also aims to bring benefits to the company. Thus, companies see their goals being achieved if the customers' needs and desires are met. Therefore, it is possible to state that sports marketing is fundamental to sustain the development of the sports industry, since it encompasses a set of actions produced to meet the needs, expectations and preferences of the consumer (Valinhas, 2010).

One of the main objectives of sports marketing is to promote and publicize sports products and services, which is why this type of marketing is mainly applied to a communications market segment. A communication strategy should mirror the objectives that the organization has previously defined. The target audience is the receiver of the message transmitted by the company, and the company must disclose both its objectives and its products. Sport can also work as a means of communication by other agents that, although they do not intervene directly in the sector as their main activity, use it in order to reach consumers or potential consumers (Sá & Sá, 2009).

The use of sport as a means of communication is a market strategy that benefits the company because it helps to build, preserve and improve the company's image and to publicize and promote its products and services, taking advantage of the wide visibility that sport has. Moreover the use of sport as a communication vehicle, is a mode of promotional marketing, i.e., it is an alternative communication of a product and/or service where the company is expecting to benefit through a sports activity of public interest (Valinhas, 2010).

The sport product offers the consumer the satisfaction of several desires or basic needs such as health, fun and sociability (Paulico, 2008). The Council of Europe, in 1992, defined sport as *"all forms of physical activities which, through organized or unorganized participation, aim at the expression or improvement of physical and mental condition, the development of social relationships or the achievement of results in competition at all levels"*.

The practice of sports activities provides benefits for our well-being and quality of life. It is also an opportunity to test our limits and potential and promote social integration. Besides all these benefits, sport is privileged in terms of psychological intervention, because as the interest in sport increases, so does the concern with performance and fitness, making sport a good example of personal competence (Dias, Cruz, & Danish, 2001). Sport is also important in the learning process because it contributes to a more coherent development of personality formation. Risk-taking, decision-making, and team spirit are a constant in the practice of any sport and may or may not preclude overly antisocial behavior in the developing child or adolescent (Sá & Sá, 2009).

In the sports market there is a huge amount of sports products and services, which makes it a very diversified market that increasingly needs the intervention of sports marketing. It is important to treat each consumer in a unique way, providing a good experience, making the customer feel an integral part of the company itself (Paulico, 2008).

2.1.2 Relationship Marketing

Relationship marketing is a form of marketing that prioritizes customer satisfaction and retention rather than sales transactions. It differs from other forms of marketing in that it recognizes the long-term value of customer relationships and extends communication beyond intrusive advertising messages. This type of marketing should be understood as a marketing strategy, where the primary focus is on maintaining a trusting relationship with the customer (Silva, Marques, Silva, & Viana, 2018).

According to Kotler (2000), relational marketing aims to build lasting mutually beneficial relationships with consumers, suppliers and distributors by ensuring good quality products, good services and fair prices. The overall satisfaction of consumers is also related to the quality of the service provided, so it is important to understand the customer's expectation in terms of quality, satisfy them and exceed that same expectation (Ferreira, 2012).

With the increase in competitiveness, advertising campaigns and sales strategies, companies seek differentiation in the product and/or service presented. Thus, with the support of relational marketing, the attitude of organizations towards customers tends to be increasingly detailed with the aim of satisfying them and consequently obtaining their loyalty (Ferreira, 2012). For, "*customer loyalty is a way to achieve greater competitiveness of companies* (Pereira, 2014). "

As reported by Leonice Martini et al (2006), consumers are well informed about the products and services offered in the market and, by forming an expectation of value, based on the information obtained, the probability of satisfaction and of new purchases depends on whether the offer matches their expectation or not. If the customer is satisfied with the product and/or service, he is more likely to remain loyal to that company for longer. Thus, relational marketing is based on producing and delivering value to the consumer, with the goal of developing stable, long-lasting, and mutually beneficial relationships for companies and customers. The longer the customer's relationship with the company, the more likely it is that the customer will remain loyal. Therefore, it is crucial to identify potential customers, differentiate them based on their needs and value to the company, and interact individually with the customer to build solid relationships. (Martini, Agostini, Rabello, Marciel, & Zanella, 2012).

High customer contact service businesses (such as gyms) should foster a friendly relationship with customers. That is, employees should act in a friendly manner toward the customer, making the customer feel good and appreciate the sociability. In this type of service, the more attention given to the customer, the more likely it is that the customer will be loyal to the company (Ferreira, 2012).

The stimulation of socialization in health clubs is a factor that should be invested in, because the social environment in these places has proven to be very important for customer retention, since health clubs with members who develop a good relationship with other users and/or employees have higher retention rates (Ferreira, 2012).

2.2 Services in the fitness industry

The service is a set of various activities, more or less tangible, between the customer and the supplier of this same service. Sports institutions have characteristics that differentiate them from other organizations that also provide services, because sports services can be considered as a superfluous luxury, because the consumption of this service can be done in leisure and free time and there is an emotional relationship created through sports activities, creating, in this way, a sense of belonging (Ferreira, 2012).

Nóbrega (1997) states that the main characteristics of services are *"intangibility, heterogeneity, presence of the client, simultaneity between production and consumption, etc".*

2.2.1 Perceived service quality

Serving customers with quality is the main goal of health clubs, for this, there should be a dedicated and organized administration so that customers are properly satisfied.

From the customer's point of view, the definition of quality is linked with excellence and with exceeding expectations. It is important to emphasize that consumers do not evaluate only the tangible aspects of the service, they also evaluate the intangible aspects such as sociability, friendliness, friendliness, etc. (Freitas, 2005).

Perceived service quality influences future purchase intentions and consequent customer retention. The perceived quality results from the comparison between the expectations and the perception created by the customer in relation to the requested service (Ferreira, 2012). There is greater customer satisfaction in organizations that can provide continuous improvements in the services provided. Extremely satisfied customers show a more loyal behavior, however, ensuring customer satisfaction does not automatically ensure customer loyalty because the customer may be attracted by a competitor. By maintaining a long term relationship with a customer, the organization will have a better understanding of the customer's preferences and needs, and in this way it will be easier to satisfy that same customer on future occasions (Ribeiro, Machado, & Tinoco, 2010).

2.3 Strategy and management in health clubs

2.3.1 Strategy

Strategic analysis is of capital importance in marketing as it allows sports organizations to fine-tune decisions and resources to competitive circumstances, opportunities, and the external and internal dynamics of the industry (Marinho, 2011).

Strategy is the way a company behaves to achieve short, medium, and long-term goals. The determination of vision, mission and objectives and the development of policies and programs to achieve these objectives are necessary elements in the development of a strategy. In other words, this concerns the complex social and economic process of conducting business involving organizational decision making.

Chandler, in 1962, defined strategy as the specification of an organization's objectives and the adoption of appropriate decisions and allocation of resources to achieve the objectives subsequently defined. In other words, when formulating a strategy it is also necessary to analyze the internal factors of the company, such as structure, production processes, and technology. (Correia, 1999).

Ansoff (1965) also defined his concept of strategy where he states that strategy is an aggregation of decision-making norms under conditions of partial development. Strategic decisions are related to the company and its ecosystem. In other words, strategy, in the view of this author, provides a common thread for the choice of the organization's relations with the outside world through its products and thus manages to strengthen the organization's potential for success (Correia, 1999).

In 1988 Mintzberg defined strategy as a mediating force between the company and the environment where it is involved, where there is a set of rules subsequently defined in the decision-making procedure to cope with the environment where it is inserted. In other words, Mintzberg focuses on the decisions and actions that are developed to respond to the environment where the organization is inserted (Nicolau, 2001).

Strategy is based on the detailed study of the variables that drive the environment of an organization, and this diversity of definitions refers that strategy concerns the future of the company, therefore in the management of organizations, the procedures for defining the objectives, the means and the ways to achieve them have to be studied as an agglomerate of integrated and coherent procedures.

In summary, it can be said that there is an organizational phenomenon that is translated by decisions with direct consequences in the resources and results obtained, whose understanding can only be obtained by analyzing the various dimensions.

In this sense, it is possible to assess in each company a certain strategy that is obtained through the organization's values and mission, an attitude towards competition, a certain positioning and a system of norms and values that provide coherence to the organization's actions (Correia, 1999).

2.3.2 Elements of strategy

The socio-economic and political aspects of the organization are becoming increasingly important, so it is necessary to respond to this environment without compromising the company's identity. There are five integral elements of strategy that are directly linked to the organization and that influence the creation of strategy.

These elements are the vocation, the vision, the mission, the strategic objectives and the opportunities and threats of the strategic environment (Vieira, 2006).

The vocation defines the purpose of the organization, that is, it defines its goal (Vieira, 2006). In other words, according to Correia (1999), *"vocation refers to the type of work that federations should do in accordance with the competence they have to intervene in a given field."*

The vision constitutes the company's strategic plan and describes the ambitions for the future without indicating how they will be achieved. From this perspective, the company's mission represents its reason for being, so the vision becomes achievable with the definition of the mission. The mission leads the company in the directions it should go, facilitating and focusing on the attitudes and actions that are intended to achieve the primary objectives. The mission determines the boundaries that serve as guidance in the implementation of strategies, determines measures for the behavior of the company and transmits the standards for the ethical conduct of the members of the organization (Costa, 2012).

Regarding the objectives of an organization, these are the purposes on which efforts should be directed. The strategic objectives enable the strengthening of the institution's main skills in the critical factors of success in the environment in which it is involved (Vieira, 2006). According to Costa (2012) objectives serve to *"organize, motivate and control actions. The mission defines directions and unspecific actions, while the objectives are attempts to make the mission tangible".* The definition of objectives has important advantages since it makes it easier to find out what the company intends to achieve, structures the decisions, directs the commitment of everyone to the defined goals, reduces the divergence of opinions in decision making and enables a continuous analysis of the company's performance (Vieira, 2006).

The analysis of the opportunities and threats of the strategic environment implies that the structural characteristics of the sector where organizations are competing and the factors of the general surrounding environment are investigated. Due to the increase in competitive processes between organizations, the traditional view of strategic analysis, where priority was given to internal aspects, was called into question (Correia, 1999). In this sense, it is possible to state that a company's success depends on the way it adapts to a concrete, structured and competitive environment (Correia, 1999). According to Porter's Five Forces model, it is important to analyze the vast rivalry between institutions, the power of buyers and suppliers, the threat of potential competitors and of substitute products and/or services. According to this model, the organization should focus on adaptive methods through the improvement of competitive advantages, whose elaboration and preservation in the long term becomes, strategically, a major issue (Correia, 1999).

2.3.3 Management in Health clubs

Sport employs millions of people worldwide, is practiced or watched by a large part of the population, and has gone from an amateur pastime to a significant sector. In this sense, it is important to emphasize that today's sport is also associated with education, health, and leisure. Taking into account the new forms of sport, it shows us new reasons for its practice, where, inevitably, the characteristics of the practitioners and the organization will be different.

In general, sports act as a form of collective expressiveness, favoring the continuous development of the human body. Therefore, administrations have great responsibility in the promotion of sports. In this way, the need for administrative grounding arises, where there can be planning, realization and evaluation with the aim of improving results in the financial, social and sporting issue (Neves, 2015).

With the increase in the number of physical activity gyms and the media's emphasis on a healthy lifestyle, there has been an increase in the public and a further evolution of health clubs. Due to this increase in the importance of physical activities and making fitness a profitable business, management has become an indispensable tool in the administration of health clubs (Furtado, 2009).

The "North American Society for Sport Management" defines sport management as:

> *"[...] an interdisciplinary grouping, which has as its characteristics the emphasis on the themes; direction, leadership and sports organization, including behavioral issues, ethics, marketing, communication, finance, economics, social responsibility, legislation and professional preparation."* (Vieira & Stucchi, 2007).

The success of any sports organization depends on the quality of strategic decisions so it is necessary to analyze the position of the organization in the competitive environment, determine the objectives and implement a strategy that matches the values and mission of the company (Hoye, Smith, Westerbeek, Stewart, & Nicholson, 2006). To do this, these organizations develop multiple behaviors daily that allow to analyze contexts and evaluate the results (Lopes, 2017).

The analysis, planning, development, and control of programs that aim to create and maintain relationships with customers are fundamental processes in the management of health clubs, as is the adaptability of the organization to the surrounding market, and conducting a prior study in order to discover what the main needs of consumers are. Organizations, in creating and expanding their products, are not only serving their customers, but are also leading a profitable campaign. For such a campaign to be successful the company should never forget the general and specific objectives determined by the defined strategy (Marinho, 2011).

Over the years there has been the need to develop new strategies, objectives, solutions and change paradigms, that is, there has been the need to seek new management methods in a sports organization because the current labor market requires new skills and new procedures that facilitate business development (Ribeiro, 2008).

The professional sports manager has been considered central to sports organizations that aspire to increase their productivity. These managers, in addition to all the responsibilities associated with their position, should also assume the responsibility of leadership. Leadership is associated with personality traits such as intelligence, influence, attitude, self-confidence, security, motivation and affinity, which enable the achievement of common goals and purposes, thus, leaders must create and maintain an internal environment that provides the excellent development of people so that it is possible to achieve the objectives of the organization (Neves, 2015).

The manager must strive to understand the needs and desires of the customers in order to ascertain, qualify and design all the advantages that can be developed and offered. In addition, the manager of a health club should know the members of his team and should highlight their attributes so that it is possible to offer the customer several activities that satisfy him and so that, in this way, it is more likely that he will be loyal to the health club. Thus, it is possible to state that the sport manager is a liaison element that is in constant relationship with people and customers in your organization (Joaquim, Batista, & Carvalho, 2011).

CHAPTER III - METHODOLOGY

3.1 Universe and Sample

The universe of this study is all gyms in the northern region of mainland Portugal, i.e., according to the 2018 Fitness Barometer in Portugal, the number of health clubs in northern mainland Portugal is 114.

The final sample consists of 346 valid questionnaires to gym users and 14 valid questionnaires to gym managers.

Below (table 1), we present the number of health clubs per district that participated in the study, as well as the number of users who correctly answered the questionnaire.

Table 1- Geographical distribution of the target population of this study, by district

	Number of Health Clubs	No. of respondents
Aveiro	2	44
Braga	2	47
Bragança	1	29
Guard	1	25
Porto	2	46
Viana do Castelo	2	53
Vila Real	2	46
Viseu	2	56
TOTALS	14	346

3.2 Data collection instruments and procedures

Two questionnaire surveys were applied to 14 gyms in the Northern region of continental Portugal, composed of eight districts, namely Aveiro, Braga, Bragança, Guarda, Porto, Vila real, Viana do Castelo and Viseu. The questionnaires were applied during the months of December 2019 and January 2020.

One questionnaire collected information from the clients, the other from the gym manager. The purpose of the study was explained to all participants, asking for their cooperation.

The questionnaire is one of the most widely used techniques for collecting data, as it allows the researcher to pose questions to the respondent for the purpose of gathering information relevant to the research.

In a first phase, a pre-test was carried out, where the first questionnaire was applied to a sample of 30 people and the second questionnaire was applied to two people in charge in order to understand if there was any difficulty in the respondents filling it out. Since this was not the case, the remaining number of gyms in the north of Portugal were then targeted for application of the same questionnaires, with no significant changes.

Before I went in person to the health club to apply the two questionnaires I sent an e-mail (appendix 1) for the purpose of asking permission to apply the questionnaires and also to explain the purpose of the study.

The first questionnaire was applied to the customers of the gym and in addition to the sociodemographic and consumer characterization questions, the questionnaire also consists of questions that had the objective of finding out how long the customer has been at the gym, its frequency, its preferences, how and how long it takes to go to the gym, the degree of satisfaction with the health club and how he got to know about it.

The second questionnaire was applied to one person in charge of each gym and this was intended to collect general information about the gym, information about marketing techniques put into practice, and information about the person in charge of the gym.

After collecting data from the entire sample, we proceeded to study the data, which was done using IBM SPSS Statistics V26 software.

3.3 Statistical Techniques

Statistical analysis and the respective data processing made it possible to give relevance to the data obtained.

Descriptive statistics were used to summarize the large data set, as well as measures of central tendency and measures of dispersion. Univariate analyses and bivariate analyses were also performed.

CHAPTER IV - HYPOTHESIS FORMULATION

H1: The degree of satisfaction regarding the cleanliness and hygiene of the gym affect positively on the customer's seniority in the health club.

Satisfaction regarding health club cleanliness is an important factor since members value the cleanliness of the facilities (Nunes, 2016) and, generally, dirt in these spaces has a negative influence on customer satisfaction (Pedragosa, 2012).

H2: The degree of satisfaction regarding the friendliness and competence of the staff positively affects the customer's weekly attendance at the health club.

Taking into account that the fitness industry is increasingly competitive, it is essential to bet on the quality of service and be attentive to the needs and demands of customers because their loyalty is influenced by the quality of service provided (Marques, 2010). It is essential to have an excellent relationship between customers and employees. Thus, the bet of the administration in the quality of employees is a strategy for members not to seek another gym (Gonçalves, Buchmann, & Carvalho, 2013).

To provide greater customer retention managers need to improve the dynamics affecting personal relationships within the health club (Ferreira, 2012).

H3: The degree of satisfaction regarding the opening hours positively influences a higher weekly customer attendance at the health club.

Customer satisfaction is critical for health clubs to secure a competitive advantage over their competition. In this sense, member satisfaction has gained greater importance from a management perspective, as it enables customer attraction and loyalty (Rocha, 2017) . In this line of thought it is important to understand if the opening hours influence the degree of customer satisfaction.

H4: The total number of Personal Trainers (PTs) in a health club positively affects satisfaction with PT instruction and follow-up.

The PT acts on participation and motivation to exercise and he/she designs the workouts to improve the client's physical and motor skills and to achieve a specific goal (Marreiros, 2014).

It is important to understand if the number of PTs influences the degree of customer satisfaction because it is possible to affirm that their satisfaction will contribute to their loyalty, turning a sporadic customer into a regular and loyal customer with a clear preference in the services of their Health Club (Rocha, 2017).

H5: The degree of satisfaction regarding the diversity of activities positively affects a higher weekly customer attendance at the health club.

Group training promotes several physical and mental advantages, and has a very beneficial socializing character, because the formation of groups becomes extremely motivating and gives rise to cohesion among clients.

In this line of thought it is important to analyze whether the satisfaction of group classes influence a higher frequency since customer satisfaction and loyalty are interconnected, and customer satisfaction is fundamental in organizations (Rocha, 2017).

H6: The degree of satisfaction regarding quality/price positively affects the number of members.

The price of the product and/or service is one of the key determinants of consumer choice. It is expected that the customer will tend to purchase a lower priced product, since the higher the price, the greater the sacrifice that its purchase will mean. However, there will be a higher perceived quality of the product if the price is higher, which will increase the customer's tendency to buy it (Abreu, 1994).

From the customer's point of view, price perception is the balance between the cost and benefit of services and the value of the monthly fee (Ferrand, Robinson, & Valette-Florence, 2010).

Price perceptions affect customer retention, so it is important that managers manage their customers' perceptions of price and the customer's perception of quality of service (Ferreira, 2012).

CHAPTER V - RESULTS

5.1 Results Obtained

The following tables show the sociodemographic and characterization information of the health club members in relation to the sample under study.

Most of the respondents in this study are male (52.02%), belong to the 21 to 40 age group (60.98%), the average age of the participants is 31.2 years and there is a standard deviation of 12.43 years. Most of them have been enrolled in the gyms for less than 6 months (33%), on average they attend the health club 3 times a week (28%), the most frequent schedule is between 5 pm and 7 pm (23%).

Table 2- Distribution of the target population of the present study, by sex

	N	%
Male	180	52,02
Female	166	47,98

Table 3- Age distribution of the target population of the study

	N	%
<=20	65	18,79
[21;40]	211	60,98
>=41	70	20,23

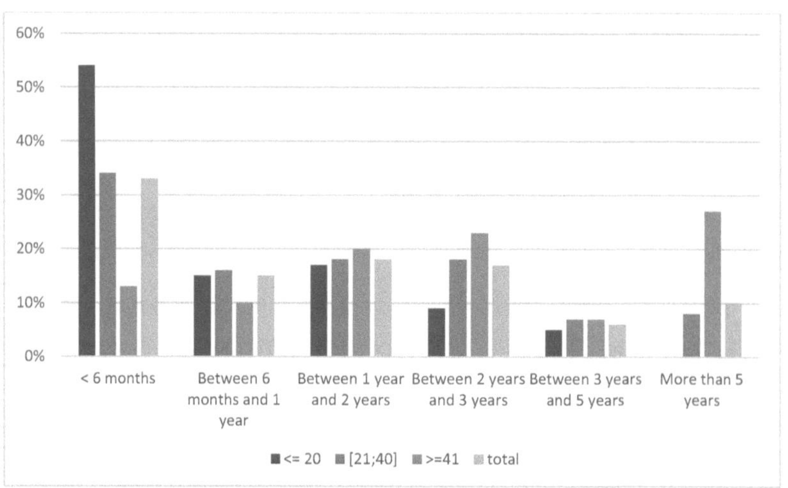

Figure 1- Health Club seniority of the study population distributed by age groups

Based on figure 1 we can conclude that the majority (54%) of respondents aged 20 or less have been enrolled for less than 6 months, the same is true for respondents who are between 21 and 40 years old (34%). However, the majority (27%) of respondents aged 41 or older have been enrolled for more than 5 years.

Frequency is directly and positively related to consumer loyalty, i.e., members who frequent the health club more are more likely to remain loyal compared to those who use the health club less (Costa, 2011). Based on the present study it can be proved that weekly attendance positively affects customer loyalty as *p-value* < 0.05. In addition, the overall customer satisfaction towards the health club influences the variables of customer loyalty (Ferreira, 2012).

In figure 2 it can be seen that respondents mostly (28%) attend the health club 3 times a week. This figure also informs that the majority (38%) of respondents aged 20 or less attend the health club three times a week. The same is true for respondents who are between 21 and 40 years old (26%). In turn, the majority (36%) of respondents over the age of 40 attend the health club only twice a week.

In this way, managers should provide more and better activities and conditions for customers to feel more satisfied so that this way there is an increase in weekly attendance and consequently the customer becomes loyal for more years with the health club.

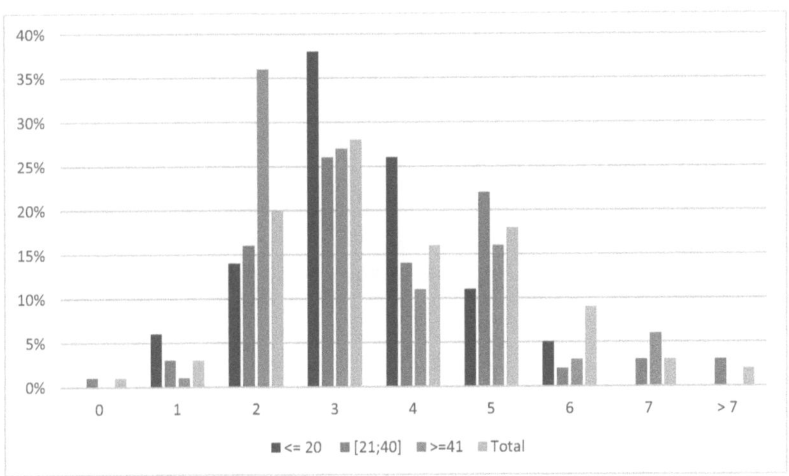

Figure 2- Weekly attendance to the health club of the study population distributed by age groups

Since, through figure 1, only 28% of the respondents under 40 years old have been enrolled in the health club for more than 2 years, managers should understand the aspects that can be improved so that these customers remain loyal to the health club for more years.

In question 6 of the first questionnaire, the participants were asked to rank from 1 (not very important) to 5 (very important) the following characteristics:

cleanliness, quality of the machines, supervision by the PTs, friendly atmosphere in the gym, and modernity of the gym.

It is possible to see in figure 3 that there are some similarities and some divergences regarding priorities and degrees of satisfaction. We can see that clients who have been enrolled for less than 6 months give more priority to cleanliness (3.3) and PT follow-up (3.3), and clients who have been enrolled for more than five years also give more importance to cleanliness (3.6) and friendly environment (3.3).

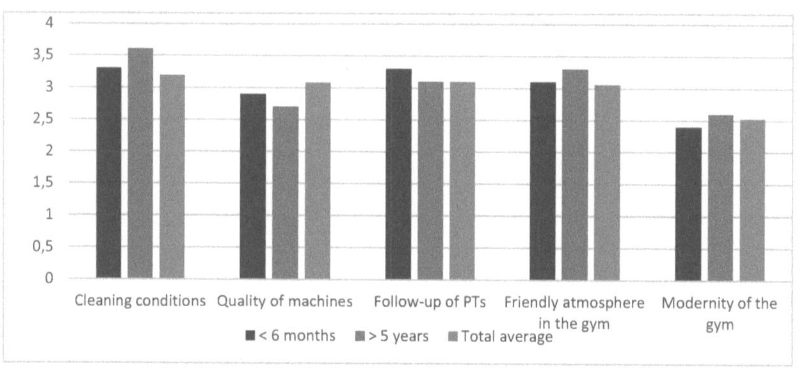

Figure 3- Preferences of the population present in the study distributed by the customer's seniority in the health club

Therefore managers should continue to invest in following up with PTs to captivate new customers, however they should also invest in the cleanliness and hygiene of the health club and in maintaining a friendly atmosphere in the gym so that customers do not leave the health club.

In question 7 of the first questionnaire the participants had to indicate their degree of satisfaction (not at all satisfied, not very satisfied, satisfied, very satisfied, and totally satisfied) regarding various parameters.

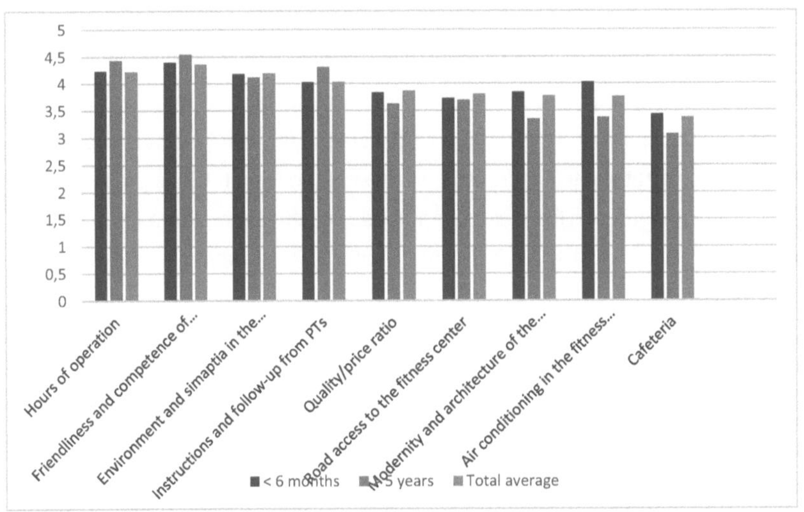

Figure 4- Level of satisfaction of the population present in the study distributed by the customer's seniority in the Health Club

It is possible to analyze in figure 4 that the respondents enrolled for less than 6 months are more satisfied with the opening hours (4.23), with the friendliness and competence of the employees (4.40) and with the environment in the gym and friendliness of the other users (4.18). Respondents enrolled for more than 5 years in the Health Club are also more satisfied with the opening hours (4.43) and the friendliness and competence of the staff (4.54) but, unlike respondents for less than 6 months, they are not as satisfied with the atmosphere in the gym and friendliness of the other users but are more satisfied with the instructions and follow-ups from the PTs (4.31).

Respondents enrolled for less than 6 months are less satisfied with the Value for money (3.83), with road access to the gym (3.73), and with the cafeteria (3.43). However, respondents enrolled for more than 5 years are less satisfied with the modernity and architecture of the gym (3.34), with the air conditioning in the gym (3.37) and also with the cafeteria (3.06).

35

Given this information managers should increase and improve the services available to customers so that in this way customers feel that the quality/price ratio is fair. They should also invest in road access, such as private parking for health club customers. They should also increase the cafeteria services so that this degree of satisfaction increases. In most of the Health Clubs present in this study the cafeteria service was only a coffee machine, i.e., there is no bar and this is a factor that makes the overall satisfaction towards the Health Club decrease.

Managers should also invest in modernizing the health club and improving the air conditioning conditions so that customer satisfaction is higher.

The number of weight-training machines influences the degree of satisfaction regarding the quality and availability of the machines. As can be seen in the following table, this degree of satisfaction is higher in health clubs that have more than 41 machines.

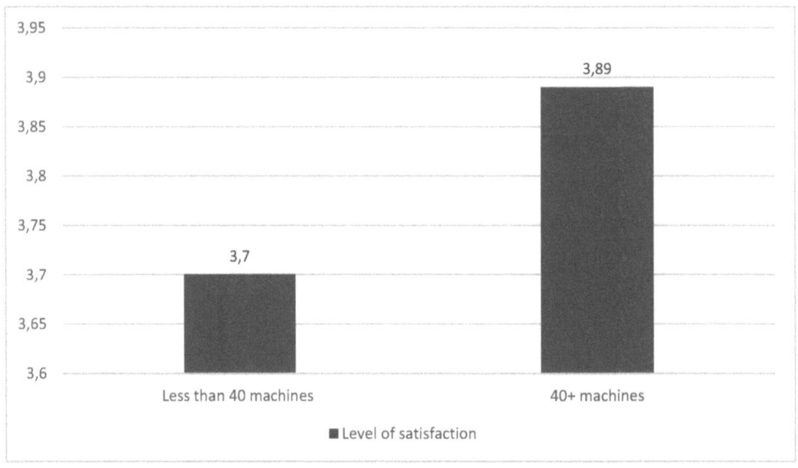

Figure 5- Satisfaction level regarding the number of weight machines at the health club

Therefore, it is important to invest in the number of bodybuilding machines, since this is a feature that influences the degree of customer satisfaction.

In these fourteen health clubs there are a total of 82 male PTs and 38 female PTs. 48.15% of the PTs are between 26 and 30 years old and 44.44% of the PTs have between 2 and 4 years of experience. It is also possible to verify that only three Health Clubs present more than 10 male PTs and only one presents more than 10 female PTs. However, no Health Club has more than 10 male and female PTs simultaneously.

Table 4- Age distribution of the PTs from the health clubs in the present study

	N	%
<=21	5	18,52
[26;30]	13	48,15
[31;35]	7	25,93
>=36	2	7,41

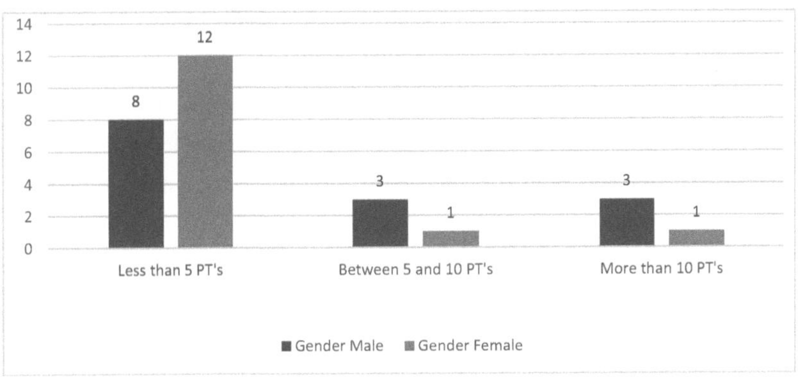

Figure 6- Number of PTs in Health Clubs

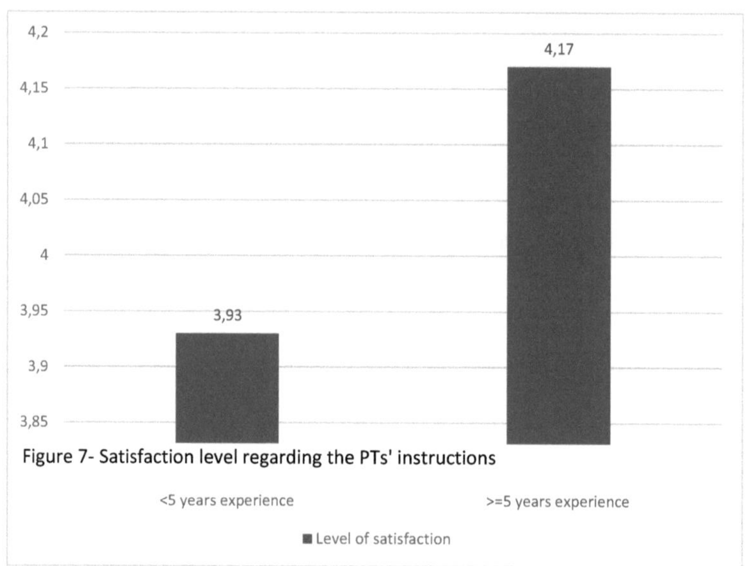

Figure 7- Satisfaction level regarding the PTs' instructions

It can be seen in figure 7 that the respondents feel more satisfied regarding the instructions and monitoring of the PTs when the PTs have more years of experience. Thus, managers should invest in PTs who have more years of experience.

Of the 14 health clubs in this study, only three do not offer discounts to new clients. The remaining Health Clubs offer certain benefits to new members, such as free first training, offer of equipment, discount on the monthly fee for the first six months, offer of the registration fee, discount on the first monthly fee, offer of registration and insurance, discount for students and family members, discount of 50% of the registration fee, and protocols with institutions.

Regarding the benefits for older customers it is possible to conclude that five health clubs practice cheaper prices for older customers, two health clubs offer a relaxing massage to the member on his birthday and also offer a monthly fee to the customer if he enrolls a friend. Two gyms offer supplements to older customers and the remaining five Health Clubs do not offer any benefits.

The majority (35.71%) of the health clubs in this study choose to offer personalized workouts in order to retain the customer in their gym. According to the answers that the managers gave in the second survey, the other ways used by the gyms to retain members are the special attention given and the daily interaction with the customer, the immediate resolution of problems, the quality of the service provided, the continuous monitoring and evaluation of the member's performance, the creation of sporting events, the offer of a discount if you opt for a loyalty contract and discounts on the monthly fee due to protocols with companies and discounts on supplements.

Most of the Health Clubs (35.71%), to attract new customers, advertise their promotions. The other campaigns made by the Health Clubs are to publicize their gym on social networks, newspapers or radio, creation of an advertising panel, offer of membership, disclosure of their campaigns where they offer sports products and one of the Health Clubs present in this study makes a raffle of trips for members.

The managers of the health clubs were also asked if new weight-training machines had already been purchased, and eight of them answered yes. Based on this answer it was asked if the acquisition of new machines had as a consequence an increase in the number of members. To this question only two said no, in other words 75% of those responsible answered that the acquisition of new bodybuilding machines increased the number of members.

All the health clubs present in this study have a coffee machine in their space, however only 3 of them have a bar. It is also possible to verify that 3 gyms provide virtual classes for members and private parking.

Regarding the people in charge of the health clubs, it is possible to analyze that there are 10 male and 4 female people in charge. Most of the people in charge (57.14%) are between 31 and 40 years old. It is also possible to verify that the majority (64%) of the people in charge of the health clubs, both male and female, have a university degree. Finally, 28.57% of the people in charge have been in charge between 1 and 5 years.

Table 5- Number of responsible persons in health clubs divided by gender

	N	%
Male	10	71,43
Female	4	28,57

Table 6- Age of the people in charge of the health clubs

	N	%
<=30	0	
[31;35]	4	28,57
[36;40]	4	28,57
[41;45]	2	14,29
[46;50]	1	7,14
[51;55]	2	14,29
>=56	1	7,14

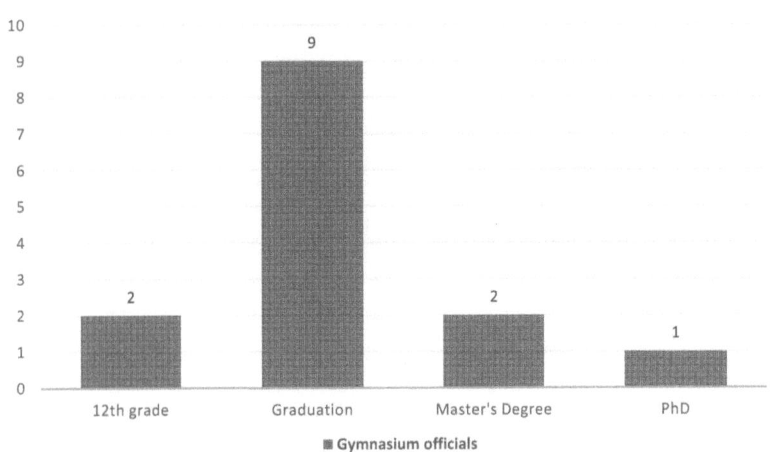

Figure 8- Degree of education of Health Club Managers

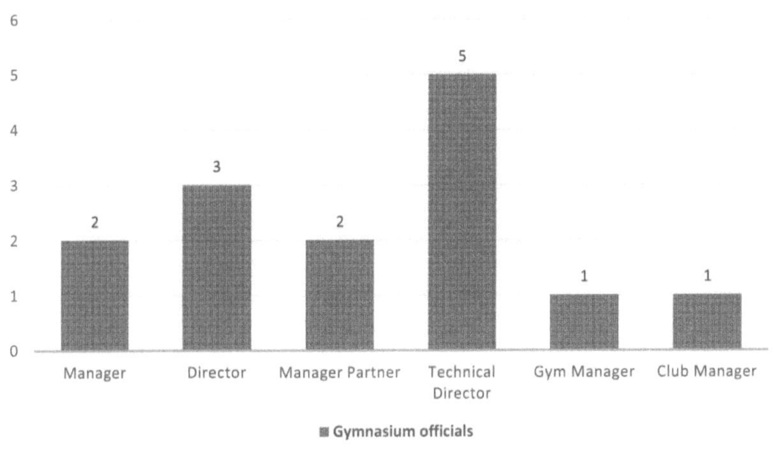

Figure 9- Role of Health Club managers

Table 7- Years of function of the people in charge of the Health Club

	N	%
<=1	2	14,29
[1;5[	4	28,57
[5;10[	3	21,43
[10;15]	3	21,43
[15;20[	0	
[20;25[	1	7,14
>=25	1	7,14

CHAPTER VI - HYPOTHESIS VALIDATION

H1 : Satisfaction regarding the cleanliness and hygiene of the gym positively affect on customer's seniority in the health club.

In this study it is found that satisfaction regarding the cleanliness and hygiene of the gym affects the seniority of the customer (*p-value* <0.05). It is also possible to analyze, based on question 6 of the first questionnaire, that the participants of this study consider the cleanliness conditions the most important parameter because it presents a mean of 3.19.

H2: The degree of satisfaction regarding the friendliness and competence of the staff positively affects the customer's weekly attendance at the health club.

When measuring the degree of satisfaction regarding the friendliness and competence of the employees, it is confirmed that this has an influence on customer frequency (*p-value* < 0.05). In view of these results it is perceptible that the relationships between employees and customers are important factors. In this line of thought, it is also important to analyze that the degree of satisfaction of the environment in the gym and friendliness of other users also has an influence on the frequency of the member in the health club (*p-value* < 0.05).

In conclusion, customer relations and employee competence are factors that influence member attendance.

H3: Satisfaction with the opening hours positively influences a higher weekly customer attendance at the health club.

It is possible to verify that satisfaction regarding the opening hours does not influence a higher frequency of the customer to the gym (*p-value* >0,05). This degree of satisfaction also does not appear to be a determinant for the customer's seniority in the gym (*p-value* >0,05).

However, it can be seen that members of the health clubs with operating hours less than 25 hours per week have, on average, a degree of satisfaction regarding operating hours of 4.02 while members of the health clubs that have weekly operating hours greater than 25 hours have a degree of satisfaction of 4.40. In other words, there is a higher degree of satisfaction in health clubs that are in operation more than 25 hours per week.

H4: The total number of PTs in a Healh Club positively affects satisfaction with PT instruction and follow-up.

In the analysis of this relationship it is possible to analyze that the total number of PTs is not significant because *p-value* >0.05.

A greater number of PTs does not automatically mean that members feel a greater satisfaction in relation to this parameter. As can be seen in table 21, there is, on average, a higher satisfaction in gyms that have seven or fewer PTs (4.07), while health clubs that have more than seven PTs have, on average, a satisfaction rating of 3.99.

However, in the case of female clients, it is possible to verify that there is a higher degree of satisfaction (4.07) in relation to the instructions and accompaniment of the PTs in the health clubs that provide more than one female PT.

Table 8- Number of PTs in the health clubs of the present study

	Degree of satisfaction
<=7	4,07
>7	3,99

Table 9- Number of female PTs in the health clubs of the present study

	Degree of satisfaction
<=1	4
>1	4,07

H5: The degree of satisfaction of the diversity of activities positively affects a higher weekly customer attendance at the health club.

The degree of satisfaction regarding the diversity of activities is a factor that influences a higher frequency (*p-value* <0.05). The total number of activities has a strong influence on this degree of satisfaction (*p-value* <0.05). It can be concluded that this degree of satisfaction also influences the seniority of the member in the health club (*p-value* < 0.05). In other words, the diversity of activities is a factor that influences both the frequency of membership and its seniority.

H6: The degree of satisfaction regarding quality/price positively affects the number of members.

When analyzing this study, it can be seen that the degree of satisfaction regarding quality/price has an influence on the number of members (*p-value* <0.05).

CHAPTER VII - CONCLUSIONS

As indicated in the third chapter, this study, which was applied in the eight northern districts of continental Portugal, aims to answer some questions that lead to customer retention in health clubs. The essential conclusions and also the limitations of this study and suggestions for future research are shown below.

Regarding the attributes provided by the Health Club, it is possible to verify that the degree of satisfaction regarding the cleanliness and hygiene of the gym positively affect the customer's seniority in the Health Club. This is an important factor, since it is the parameter to which customers give more importance. Thus, it is important that the health club manager makes sure that the gym is clean and tidy. It is also possible to verify that the degree of satisfaction regarding the opening hours does not positively affect the customer's frequency and seniority in the Health Club. However, in this study, the customers of health clubs that have an opening hours of more than 25 hours per week show a higher degree of satisfaction regarding the opening hours than the customers of health clubs that have an opening hours of less than 25 hours per week. Regarding the number of PTs, it can be analyzed that a higher number of PTs does not automatically mean that the members feel a higher satisfaction regarding the satisfaction regarding the instructions and follow-up of the PTs. But it is important to invest in female PTs because the degree of satisfaction regarding PT instruction and follow-up increases in health clubs that have more than one female PT. It is also important to invest in PTs with more years of experience since the degree of satisfaction of the respondents regarding the instructions and accompaniment of the PTs is higher in the health clubs that have more experienced PTs. Another factor that managers can invest in is the diversity of activities, because it is possible to conclude that the total number of activities has a strong influence on the degree of satisfaction of the diversity of activities. And this degree of satisfaction positively influences the frequency and seniority of the member. Managers should strive to keep the balance of quality/price balanced, because the degree of satisfaction regarding quality/price positively affects a greater number of members.

Regarding the environment and competence of the employees, it can be seen that it is crucial to maintain a friendly atmosphere in the gym and invest in competent employees because these are two factors that positively affect the attendance of customers at the health club.

Regarding the accessory attributes it is possible to verify that managers may also invest in the cafeteria, in road access, in a greater number of machines and in the modernization of the gym so that in this way the customer satisfaction increases and consequently also increase the frequency of visits to the gym, which in this way will increase the chances of a customer becoming loyal for more years with the respective health club.

There are limitations related to the nature of the research, namely the number of the sample, since, in future research it would be important to increase the number of respondents per health club. It is also important that, in future research, the sample number be expanded to the national level.

In future research it is important to include in the customer questionnaire questions related to the reason for leaving the previous gym, in order to understand the characteristics that members give more importance. It is important to include more questions related to the degree of customer satisfaction with the management and staff to understand how this parameter influences the frequency and seniority of the customer.

Another point that would also be important to study in future research is the influence of digital media on the management and interaction of managers with customers. Digital media are currently present in the daily lives of individuals and especially in the younger population and these digital media facilitate the sharing of progress regarding physical activity in the health club (Depper & Howe, 2017). Moreover, thanks to digital media, it is also possible for a health club to offer virtual classes where the customer does not need to leave home. Thus, it is crucial to analyze in future research how digital marketing can be a competitive advantage.

Finally, it is also important, in addition to providing a good quality service, to incorporate the financial, commercial, and operational area to achieve better retention rates and profit margins.

BIBLIOGRAPHIC REFERENCES

Abreu, C. (1994). Consumer behavior before sales promotion: a study of the price-perceived quality relationship. *Revista de Administração de Empresas*, V.34, n.4, p. 64-73 Available at: http://www.scielo.br/pdf/rae/v34n4/a08v34n4.pdf?fbclid=IwAR0vuLAcYN qVMD0sPdVOoW4F04GYNwJdeRctkvHXLuRctLLaHZCS5FSfuH0.

Afif, A. (2000). A Bola da Vez: o marketing esportivo como estratégia de sucesso. *São Paulo: Infinito Carneiro, A. (2008). But after all, what is Marketing? Portal da Administração.*

Association, A. M. (2017). *Definitions of Marketing.* Obtido de https://www.ama.org/the-definition-of-marketing-what-is-marketing/ (12-12-2019)

Cardoso, O. R. (1995). Focusing total service quality on the extended product concept. *Tese de doutoramento. Brazil: Federal University of Santa Catarina - Department of Production and Systems Engineering.*

European Charter for Sport. (1992). Available at: http://www.idesporto.pt/DATA/DOCS/LEGISLACAO/Doc120.pdf.

Churchill Jr, G., & Peter, J. (2017). *Marketing - Creating value for customers. 3rd Edition.* São Paulo: Saraiva.

Correia, A. (1999). Estratégia das Federações Desportivas: Estudo das principais federações portuguesas no ciclo olímpico de 1993 a 1996. *Tese Doctoramento. Lisboa: Universidade Técnica de Lisboa - Faculdade da Motricidade Humana.*

Costa, A. (2012). Strategies of Sport Organizations. The Great Ideological Guidelines of Strategic Orientation of the International Olympic Committee: from Athens (1896) to Beijing (2008). *Tese de doutoramento. Lisbon: Technical University of Lisbon - Faculty of Human Motricity.*

Costa, R. (2011). Determinants of Customer Loyalty in Health & Fitness . Dissertação *de mestrado, Lisboa: Faculdade de Motricidade Humana - Universidade Técnica de Lisboa.*

Depper, A., & Howe, D. (2017). Are we fit yet? English adolescent girl's experiences of health and fitness apps. *Healt Sociology review (pp. 98-112) v.26 nº1.* Disponível em: https://www.tandfonline.com/doi/abs/10.1080/14461242.2016.1196599?j ournalCode=rhsr20.

Dias, C., Cruz, J., & Danish, S. (2001). Sport as a context for learning and teaching life skills: Intervention programs for children and adolescents. *Análise Psicológica v.19 nº1 pp. 157-170.* Lisboa. V.1 XIX: Available at: http://www.scielo.mec.pt/scielo.php?script=sci_arttext&pid=S0870-82312001000100013.

Dias, I. (1992). Some observations on contribution margin. *Journal of business administration,* 36-45. Available at: http://www.scielo.br/pdf/rae/v32n3/a05v32n3.pdf.

Fernandes, S., & Pereira, B. (2006). A prática desportiva dos jovens e a sua importância na aquisição de hábitos de vida saudáveis. Lisbon, Portugal: Lidel-Edições Técnicas.

Ferrand, A., Robinson, L., & Valette-Florence, P. (2010). The Intention-to-Repurchase Paradox: A Case of the Health and Fitness Industry. *Journal of Sport Management,* v.24 nº1 p. 83-105 DOI: 10.1123/jsm.24.1.83.

Ferreira, B., Marques, H., Caetano, J., Rasquilha, L., & Rodrigues, M. (2015). *Fundamentos de Marketing.* Portugal, Lisboa: Edições Sílabo.

Ferreira, C. (2012). A study on customer loyalty and retention in the fitness area. *Dissertação de mestrado. Castelo Branco: Instituto Politécnico de Castelo Branco - Escola Superior de Gestão.*

Freitas, A. (2005). Quality in services in the context of competitiveness v5, nº1. *Revista produção online.* Florianópolis, Brazil: Available at: https://producaoonline.org.br/rpo/article/view/321/418.

Furtado, R. (2009). From Fitness to Wellnes: The three concepts of gym development. *Pensar a Prática.* Brazil, V.12 n.1 p.1-11: Available at: https://www.revistas.ufg.br/fef/article/view/4862/5345.

Gonçalves, C., Buchmann, C., & Carvalho, M. (2013). Percecion of service quality and member satisfaction in fitness: Contributions to the manager's role. *Intercontinental Journal of Sport Management,* Vol. 3, suppl. 2, pp. 47-58. Available at: https://bibliotecadigital.ipb.pt/bitstream/10198/9111/1/RIGD_2013.pdf.

Hoye, R., Smith, A., Westerbeek, H., Stewart, B., & Nicholson, M. (2006). *Sport Management: Principles and Applications.* 5ª Edição. Holanda: Elsevier.

Joaquim, B., Batista, P., & Carvalho, M. (2011). Systematic Review on the competence profile of the sport manager (pp. 255-279). *Movimento: Journal of the school of physical education.* Brazil, V. 17 n.1 p.256-279: Available at: https://www.researchgate.net/publication/237022997_Revisao_Sistematica_sobre_o_perfil_de_competencias_do_gestor_desportivo.

Junior, C., Bruni, A., Paixão, R., & Filho, N. (2009). Uso da margem de contribuição em controladoria: Um estudo de caso em empresa de transporte urbano de passageiro. *Revista de Contabilidade do Mestrado em Ciências Contábeis da UERJ*, 2-17. Retrieved from https://www.e-publicacoes.uerj.br/index.php/rcmccuerj/article/view/5525/4014.

Kitchen, P., & Moss, D. (1995). Marketing and Public Relations: An Exploratory Study. *The World Association of Research Professionals*. Amsterdão, Holanda.

Kotler, P. (2000). *Marketing management, millenium Edition. 10ª Edição.* New Jersey: Prentice hall.

Londrevie, J., Dionísio, P., Denis, L., & Rodrigues, V. (1996). Mercator - Teoria e Prática. p. 6ª Edição. Lisboa: Gestão e Inovação: Ciências de Gestão.

Lopes, A., Matos, E., & Moraes, R. (1999). Modelo de decisão de preço de venda - um estudo exploratório. In: VI Congresso Brasileiro de Custos, São Paulo, Brazil Available at: https://anaiscbc.emnuvens.com.br/anais/article/viewFile/3152/3152.

Marine, I. (2011). Marketing as a strategic tool in the study of gym and health club total fitness. *Master's dissertation. Porto: Faculdade de desporto - Universidade do Porto.*

Marques, D. (2010). Avaliação da qualidade do serviço nos ginásios. *Lisboa: Instituto Universitário de Lisboa, Iscte Business School.*

Marreiros, F. (2014). Analysis of the association between professional experience, clients' perception of motivation and motivational strategies used by personal trainers. *Lisboa: Faculdade de Educação Física e Desporto, UNIVERSIDADE LUSÓFONA DE HUMANIDADES E TECNOLOGIAS.*

Martini, L., Agostini, M., Rabello, G., Marciel, A., & Zanella, W. (2012). Relationship marketing: a case study in a Travel Agency in the North. p. doi: 10.18226/35353535.v1.2012.14.

Moorman, C., Heerde, H., Moreau, P., & Palmatier, R. (2019). Challenging the Boundaries of Marketing. *Journal of Marketing.* V83, nº5, p.1-4: doi: 10.1177/0022242919867086.

Moreira, A., Cardadeiro, E., & Pedragosa, V. (2016). Fitness Barometer in Portugal. *How Are Portuguese Gyms Doing? The information most sought after by gym owners.*

Neves, T. (2015). Functional profile of the Technical Director of Health. Master's thesis. *Évora: School of Sciences and Technology, University of Évora.*

Nicolau, I. (2001). O Conceito de Estratégia. Lisboa: Instituto para o Desenvolvimento da Gestão Empresarial: Available at: https://student.dei.uc.pt/~nfnt/conceito%20estrategia.pdf.

Nóbrega, K. (1997). Quality management in services. *Tese de doutoramento, Brasil: Escola Politécnica da Universidade de São Paulo.*

Nunes, A. (2016). Members' perceptions of the quality of special programs at the Portuguese gymnasium club. Master's dissertation. *Lisboa: Faculdade de educação Física e Desporto, Universiade Lusófona de Humanidades e Tecnologias.*

Paulico, F. (2008). *Sports marketing on the podium. Gestin, 7: 113-121.*

Pedragosa, V. (2012). Satisfação e Fidelizaçao em Ginásios e Health Clubs: Estudo das Expetativas, das emoções e da Qualidade. *Lisboa: Faculdade de Motricidade Humana, Universidade Técnica de Lisboa.*

Pedragosa, V., & Cardadeiro, E. (2018). Fitness barometer in Portugal.

Pelsmacker, P., Geuens, M., & Bergh, J. (2010). *Marketing Communications: A European Perspective.* 4ª Edição. Inglaterra: Pearson Education Limited.

Pereira, C. (2014). A importância do marketing relacional nas Instituições de Ensino Superior Politécnico Público: o caso da ESTeSC. *Master's thesis. Coimbra: Oliveira do Hospital School of Technology and Management.*

Ribeiro, J., Machado, C., & Tinoco, M. (2010). Determinants of satisfaction and quality attributes in banking services. *Gestão & Produção pp. 775-790 v.17 nº4.* São Carlos, Brazil: Available at: http://www.scielo.br/scielo.php?pid=S0104-530X2010000400011&script=sci_arttext.

Ribeiro, S. (2008). Perspectivas de atuação do profissional de educação física: Perfil de habilidades no atual contexto de mercado e formação inicial. *XII Encontro Latino Americano de Iniciação Científica e VIII Encontro Latino Americano de Pós-Graduação - Universidade do Vale do Paraíba.* Brazil: Available at: http://www.inicepg.univap.br/cd/INIC_2008/anais/arquivosCEGLU/CEGL U1695_01_A.pdf.

Rocha, I. (2017). Satisfaction and customer loyalty in the fitness area. *Porto: Instituto Superior de Contabilidade e Administração do Porto.*

Rowley, J. (1998). *Library Review: Promotion and marketing communications in the iformation marketplace (pp.383).* V. 47, nº8. Inglaterra: Emerald Group Publishing Limited.

Sá, D., & Sá, C. (2009). *Marketing for sport: a business game*. Porto, Portugal: Edições IPAM.

Sá, D., & Sá, C. (2009). *Sports Marketing: The new rules of the game*. Porto, Portugal: Edições IPAM.

Sepp, C., Manfroi, L., Theisen, C. P., Diel, E. H., & Diel, F. J. (2015). SALES PRICE FORMATION: A STUDY APPLIED IN A RESTAURANT IN THE MUNICIPALITY OF CHAPECÓ- SC. *Revista tecnológica. Brasil.*

Silva, A., Marques, E., Silva, M., & Viana, S. (2018). Relationship marketing through Customer Relationship Management (CRM) as a loyalty building strategy. *Revista Internacional de Apoyo a la Inclusión, Logopedia, Sociedad y Multiculturalid (pp.107-118)*. Spain, v.4 no.1: Available at: https://doi.org/10.17561/riai.v4.n1.7.

Valinhas, B. (2010). Marketing do desporto modalidades pouco mediáticas estudo de caso volleibol Sport Lisboa e Benfica. *Master's dissertation. Lisbon: Instituto Superior de Ciências Sociais e Políticas - Universidade Técnica de Lisboa*, pp. 10-15.

Vieira, P. (2006). Estratégia das organizações desportivas - Estudo de caso: Porto Handball Association. *Monografia. Porto: Faculty of Sports - University of Porto.*

Vieira, T., & Stucchi, S. (2007). Preliminary Relationships Between Sport Management and the Physical Education Professional. *Revista da Faculdade de Educação Física da UNICAMP (pp. 113-128)*. Brazil, V. 5 n. 2: Available at: https://doi.org/10.20396/conex.v5i2.8637882.

Weitz, B., & Bradford, K. (1999). Personal Selling and Sales Management: A Relationship Marketing Perspective. *Journal of the Academy of Marketing Science (pp.241-254)*. Estados Unidos da América, v. 27(2): Disponível em:
https://www.academia.edu/28230977/Personal_Selling_and_Sales_Man agement_A_Relationship_Marketing_Perspective.

Zamberlan, L. (2008). *Pesquisa de mercado*. Ijuí, Rio Grande Do Sul, Brazil: Editora Unijuí.

APPENDICES

APPENDIX 1

E-mail explaining the purpose of the study

As part of the 9th edition of the Master in Sports Management and Direction of the University of Évora, I am developing a research project, whose project was approved by the Scientific Council, on the analysis of management strategies of Health Clubs in the northern region of Portugal.

The purpose of this study is to obtain relevant information through surveys that will be done to the managing bodies and users of gyms in Portugal in order to collect information to understand which are (1) the marketing and profitability strategies of the gyms; (2) the geographical characteristics and access to the gyms; (3) the training methodologies put into practice; (4) other ancillary attributes aimed at pleasing the customer.

For this purpose, we have requested the important collaboration of a gym manager in this study by individually answering the questionnaire (sent in attachment), so I would like to schedule an appointment with you to apply the questionnaire next week (I will come there personally). I would also like to ask if you would allow me to administer another short questionnaire (also sent in attachment) to the users of your gym to get information about their preferences.

All your answers and the name of the gym will be strictly confidential and decisive for the success of the investigation.

I will be happy to share the final results of the study with all those who participated in completing the questionnaire, so that these statistical results can also be applied by the management bodies of your gym.

Best regards,

João Pereira

Student of the Master's degree course in Sports Management and Direction of the University of Évora.

I want morebooks!

Buy your books fast and straightforward online - at one of world's fastest growing online book stores! Environmentally sound due to Print-on-Demand technologies.

Buy your books online at
www.morebooks.shop

Kaufen Sie Ihre Bücher schnell und unkompliziert online – auf einer der am schnellsten wachsenden Buchhandelsplattformen weltweit! Dank Print-On-Demand umwelt- und ressourcenschonend produzi ert.

Bücher schneller online kaufen
www.morebooks.shop

KS OmniScriptum Publishing
Brivibas gatve 197
LV-1039 Riga, Latvia
Telefax: +371 686 204 55

info@omniscriptum.com
www.omniscriptum.com

MIX
Papier aus verantwortungsvollen Quellen
Paper from responsible sources
FSC® C105338
FSC
www.fsc.org

Printed by Books on Demand GmbH, Norderstedt / Germany